HOW TO CONSUMER COURT

A DO-IT-YOURSELF GUIDE ON NAVIGATING INDIAN CONSUMER COURTS

VIJAY KAPOOR

ISBN 979-888503951-2

To

elders and teachers

Contents

Acknowledgements — vii

Disclaimer — ix

About The Author — xi

Preface — xiii

PART ONE

1. Before You Begin — 3

2. Before You Start Your Campaign — 5

3. Some Central Features Of The Cp Act — 7

4. Additional Support For Your Campaign — 10

PART TWO

5. How To Write Your Complaint — 21

6. Admission Of The Complaint By The Court — 25

7. Written Statement By The Opposite Parties — 26

8. Filing Of Affidavit-in-evidence — 27

9. Affidavit-in-evidence By The Opposite Party — 32

10. Written Arguments Of Complainant — 33

11. Written Arguments By The Opposite Party — 38

PART THREE

12. Be Forewarned And Forearmed — 41

13. What To Do In The Event Of ...... — 47

14. A Few Rx Observations — 49

Acknowledgements

Secretarial assistance, proof-reading, cover design, and for putting it up for publication, the services provided by M/s. Notion Press are gratefully acknowledged.

Disclaimer

This book is written by a layman for the layman. It is intended to be supplemental. Litigants should seek subject professional guidance.

About The Author

Although the author is an MBA type, he mostly is a jack-of all and master-of-none. His current status in life is uncertain, but he retired as the Head of Research and Chief Technical Analyst of Markets in a prominent stock broking firm in India. His first employment was as a banker in Canada from whence he is known to have been sacked. He met a similar fate as Divisional Manager of the Steel Mill Division of a corporation in Mumbai. The author does not confirm but we are certain that in his next position as Marketing Manager in a major corporate house in Mumbai, he was embroiled in a six year long drawn out battle with the top brass, from where he emerged semi-victorious. He wishes to record here his grateful thanks to the Chairman of the said corporation for the unhindered opportunity to stand his ground and do battle with his seniors to prove his point without being summarily dismissed.

The author is a man of diverse interests and bears many scars as, for instance, when he was caught cheating in a grade ten exam, and the full measure of six canings was deployed to his person, or when that (or those?) bird pitilessly flew away from his reach.

It is a widely held belief that the past is the surest predictor of the future and, so it is not out of character for the author, if he is not engaging with his seniors, to cross swords with entities before consumer courts. It is not implausible, therefore, that this book emerges from that narrative and, whence, like Mr. Jeff Bezos, the author hopes to earn a penny or two. However, one may hasten to add that, unlike the said Mr. Bezos who recently was able to taste a space journey, the author merely endeavours for a director's seat in heaven or thereabouts, and enquires of his readers whether that is at all an unreasonable wish.

Preface

There are times when one gets rankled. It could be because of something as quotidian as when you tendered a hundred rupee note for an item that cost ninety nine rupees and the establishment did not give you back the balance one rupee for want of "change". Or it could be because of something big as when a builder refuses or otherwise fails to register in your name the apartment you purchased from him. There are many shades in between: maybe the workshop didn't fix your car right, or an item that you purchased from an e-commerce entity turned out to be defective or different from what was advertised.

So, what to do?

In most instances of petty annoyances it may not be a bad idea to adopt a suitable version of grin-and-bear-it. However, when the issue is of sufficient importance for you to want a formal resolution, there are options to choose from. One of which options is to go the route of consumer courts under The Consumer Protection Act, 2019, here after referred to as the Act or CP Act.

The advantages of going the CP Act route are that it is simple to the extent that it is shorn of almost all provisions of complicated laws or codes, such as The Civil Proccedure Code, The Evidence Act and, hence, one can handle the matter oneself, although it is advised to engage a professional to represent you. The court fees vary from NIL to very little, depending upon the claim value. And, at least in theory, adjournments are not allowed except under mitigating circumstances, and the matter is to be decided within three or five months of receipt of notice by the opposite party, depending upon whether or not there is a need to conduct a laboratory test for a product in question.

I am not a lawyer, or even a lawyerly type. I have "learnt" law over the years through print media and Tv reports, and have perused some texts on the subject. Over the last fifty odd years I have instituted and / or argued myself some thirteen cases in different courts, out of which I have so far succeeded in seven, lost one, and five are pending adjudication. This book is based on my experiences in courtrooms as a "practising layman". I hope that it will be of some assistance to you.

PART ONE

CHAPTER ONE

Before you begin

In my experience, the consumer courts will typically take at least three months to adjudicate a matter. It is, however, better to budget for a longer time horizon. It will require upto ten visits to court, give or take a few: the first visit for filing the complaint, another for deciding by the court on its admissibility, a third visit to receive the opposite party's Reply, a possible fourth visit in the event the opposite party does not file its Reply at the first opportunity, a fifth visit for you to file your Affidavit Evidence, a sixth one to receive the opposite party's Affidavit Evidence, a seventh one to file your Written Arguments, and an eighth one to receive the opposite party's Written Arguments, a ninth visit for you and the opposite party to make their Oral Arguments. And you are done!

It is important that you should take a moment or two to take a deep breath and ponder. Are you still feeling so "injured" as to haul the opposite party over the coals? Does the matter justify allocation of your resources in terms of time and expenses? Should you engage a lawyer or argue the matter by yourself, and so on.

At this stage one may also want to consider some other available non-adversarial options: There is a Consumer Conciliation Committee, usually under the local ministry of

Civil Supplies. It lacks legal teeth but tries to persuade the opposing parties to amicably settle their disputes. There are no fees. It will take about four visits for an outcome this or that way. The resolution rate or the bark-to-bite ratio may only be about 10 or 20%, but it may be worth trying. There is yet another option offered by the Government of India portal https://www.consumerhelpline.gov.in/ that offers a digital platform for the resolution of complaints. It is free, and one can take advantage of the platform from the comfort of one's home without having to make any visits to anywhere.

However, once you have arrived at the conclusion that doing battle is the only way forward, you are ready to prepare for and launch your campaign.

CHAPTER TWO

Before you start your campaign

Before you start your campaign, you will need some gear, a kit.

1. Get hold of a copy of the Consumer Protection Act, 2019. The bare version of it is available for around Rs. 100 from book stores selling law books. Otherwise it can also be purchased from online e-retailers. Somewhat more informative is the version commonly referred to as the CP Act with a commentary. It has additional information, guidelines, and case laws. It starts at around Rs. 500 and can go upto a few thousand;

2. Acquaint yourself with the broad contours of law. You can do this by perusing the legal section of your newspaper, or the occasional reporting on Tv channels, or by perusing some web-portals like LiveLaw, The Wire, Scroll.in, The Quint, indiankanoon.org, etc.;

3. Visit https://confonet.nic.in/, a Government of India portal for status / proceedings of consumer complaints across all consumer courts across India, and familiarise

yourself with the court process / proceedings by accessing any random consumer complaint number as per the specified format;

4. Do some internet research. Just type in something like, "SC on consumer complaints", or "consumer court judgments", or "SC in XYZ vs. ABC", and so on. There will be a number of judgments / discussions which one should peruse and imbibe;

5. Put together of all evidence documents that you may have in your possession, such as invoices, correspondence, brochures, and whatever else that is material;

6. It is important and mandatory for you to first send a legal notice to the opposite party by registered acknowledgement due post. This can also be done by email or by Whats App, provided the opposite party is in correspondence with you via this media. The legal notice should be a brief outline of the unresolved issues, your efforts to resolve same, and a request to settle the matter by making good the price, product, service within x number of days, failing which you would be obliged to seek legal redress at their entire cost, expense, damages, and consequences.

CHAPTER THREE

Some central features of the CP Act

- Is applicable to Deficiency – Defect and Unfair Trade Practice relating to goods and services;

- Is applicable to any consumer of goods and services. Please note that a consumer is one who avails the goods or services for personal use only or for the purpose of making a livelihood by self-employment. Goods and services availed of by a person or entity for commercial purposes does not classify as a consumer;

- E-commerce entities are now firmly brought under the CP Act;

- The complaint should be filed within two years from the date on which the cause of action arose;

- A consumer can institute a complaint within the local jurisdiction of where the complainant resides or works, or where the opposite party resides or carries on business or has a branch office or personally works for gain, or where the cause of action wholly or in part arises;

- Court fees range in gradations from NIL for claims upto rupees five lakh before the district consumer courts, to Rs. 7500 for claims above rupees ten crores before the National Consumer Court;

- The provisions of the Civil Procedure Code, except those provisions that are specifically mentioned in the CP Act, do not apply to the proceedings under the CP Act, so also the provisions of The Evidence Act also do not apply. In other, words, the CP Act is sort of a code in itself where matters are to be adjudicated along the lines of natural justice;

- The provisions of the CP Act are in addition to and not in derogation to the provisions of any other law;

- Every complaint should be disposed of by the consumer court as expeditiously as possible within a period of three months from the date of receipt of notice by the opposite party where the complaint does not require analysis or testing of commodities and within five months if it requires analysis or testing of commodities;

- No adjournment shall ordinarily be granted by the district consumer court unless sufficient cause is shown and the reasons for grant of adjournment have been recorded in writing and shall make such orders as to the costs occasioned by the adjournment as may be specified by regulations;

- The district consumer court is to settle the consumer dispute on the basis of evidence brought to its notice by the complainant and the opposite party, or ex-parte on the basis of evidence brought to its notice by the complainant if the opposite party omits or fails to take any action to represent his case, or decide the complaint on merits if the complainant fails to appear on the date of hearing;

- The consumer courts have the powers, amongst other things, to direct the opposite party to replace the goods, refund the purchase price with interest, compensate the consumer for any loss or injury suffered due to the negligence of the opposite party, compensate the consumer with punitive damages, remove the defects in goods or deficiencies in service, issue corrective advertisement, and so on;

- Cases filed by or against the senior citizens, physically challenged, widows, and persons suffering from serious ailments are to be listed and disposed off on a priority basis;

- An appeal against the order of the District Commission to the State Commission is to be lodged within forty-five days from the date of the order by the District Commission. An appeal against the order of the State Commission to the National Commission is to be lodged within thirty days from the date of the order by the State Commission.

CHAPTER FOUR

Additional support for your campaign

It is a common belief that the word, the written word (codes, Acts, laws, agreements, discussions, expressions, orders, judgments, assessments, emotions, averments, descriptions, or whatever), is an adequate or even a satisfying mirror image of the whatever. It may so hurt our sensibilities but, unfortunately, this belief is unfounded.

It is true that in many, but not in all or even in most, instances the written word is superior in capturing the complete authenticity / historicity / applicability of a subject matter or of the whatever. So we have laws that are put down in the form of the written word, as in codes, laws, regulations, Acts, or whatever. However, because the written word is itself not a perfect instrument, the courts better interpret the various provisions of laws that are questioned or are challenged, and pass clarificatory "orders" or "judgments". The provisions of such orders or judgements when passed by the higher courts after due deliberations and reasoning, and not otherwise, have the effect of becoming "precedent" law, that sometimes fine-tune or even supersede the actual written law or code. Hence, such judgments could be a very important instruments in your armoury. A few such are listed here below for easy reference, and where SC = Supreme Court; NC = National Commission; HC = High Court, SCC = State Consumer Commission; DCC = District Consumer Court:

- DCC (Ferozepur): Lakhbir Singh vs. Aman Arora Telecom .... it is advantage consumer;

- NC: Y. Yasodhamma vs. The Supdt. Of Prohibition & Excise .... the provisions of the CP Act have to be construed in favour of the consumer;

- NC: Sheela Ohri vs. Bajaj Allianz .... the provisions of the CPC, except where specifically permitted under the CPAct, will have no application;

- NC: Maruti Udyog vs. Bhawana Sabharwal .... the consumer forum is to protect the interest of the consumer and can grant relief on the basis of the facts in the complaint considering the overall circumstances of the case;

- NC: Delhi Development Authority vs. DC Sharma ...... should recover the damages amount from the salaries of the delinquent officials who have been pursuing meritless litigation;

- NC: Chandrakant Kadam vs. Asst. Engineer, MSEB, Atpadi .... we would enhance the compensation to Rs. 33,500/- @ Rs. 500/- for each day the electricity remained disconnected which amount shall be recovered by the department from its negligent and defaulting officials;

- SC: India Photographic Ltd. Vs. HD Shourie .... rational approach and not a technical approach is the mandate of the CP Act;

- SC: New India Assurance Ltd. Vs. R. Srinivasan ..... every procedure is to be understood as permissible till it is shown to be prohibited by the law ..... the interest of justice cannot be defeated by rule of technicality, the rules of procedure, as has been laid down by this court a number of times, are intended to serve the ends of justice and not to defeat the dispensation of justice;

- NC: Geeta Jethani vs. Airport Authority of India .... under the CP Act the matters are to be decided *dehors* of all technicalities developed under the civil / criminal jurisprudence, and the procedure prescribed under the CP Act does not provide for application of Evidence Act or the Civil Procedure Code, and the dispute is to be decided on the yardstick of reasonable probability on the basis of facts brought on record;

- SC: Savita Garg vs. National Heart Institute .... the consumer fora not to short circuit the matter or defeat the claim on technical grounds;

- SC: Charan Singh vs. Healing Touch Hospital .... CP Act is one of the benevolent pieces of legislation intended to protect a large body of consumers from exploitation. The Act provides for an alternative system of consumer justice by summary trial ..... the consumer fora are required to consider not only the alleged harm or mental pain, agony or physical discomfort, loss of salary and emoluments, etc. suffered by the consumer but also the quality of conduct committed by the opposite party in case of proven negligence;

- SC: Sunil Kohli vs. M/s Purearth Infrastructure Ltd. ...... if the commercial use is by the purchaser himself for the purpose of earning his livelihood by means of self-employment, such purchaser of goods is yet a "consumer";

- SC: M/s. Imperia Structures Ltd. Vs. Anil Patni ...... insofar as cases where such proceedings under the CP Act are initiated after the provisions of the RERA Act came into force, there is nothing in the RERA Act which bars such initiation ... it is the discretion of the allottee whether he appropriates proceedings under the CP Act or he files an application under the RERA Act ;

- SC: Biman Bose vs. United India Insurance Ltd., ... what we find is that arbitrariness is writ large in the actions of the respondent company when it refused to renew the mediclaim policy of the insured on the ground of his past conduct i.e. having gone into litigation for payment of his claim .... if we take the view that the Mediclaim policy cannot be renewed with retrospective effect, it would give handle to the insurance company to refuse the renewal of the policy on extraneous consideration .... the insurance company argued that since the appellant has not deposited the premium for subsequent years, the policy cannot be renewed with retrospective effect. It is not disputed that the appellant sent a cheque for Rs. 1.796/- towards premium but the same was returned to the appellant. Thereafter, the parties had been litigating and respondent insurance company stopped having any correspondence with the appellant. Therefore, there arose no occasion for the appellant to deposit the premium;

- SC: V. Krishana Rao vs. Nikhil Super Specialty Hospital ...... complaints before a consumer fora are tried summarily following the principles of natural justice, and Evidence Act, 1872 is not applicable;

- HC (Delhi) Mukat Lal Duggal vs. United India Insurance Ltd. ..... the expression, "policy may be renewed by mutual consent" and "the company may at any time cancel this policy" occurring in the prospectus cannot be resorted to by these Government Companies for urging that they can arbitrarily put an end to the Mediclaim policy or arbitrarily refuse to accept renewal premium which is tendered in time. These Government Companies being "State" under Article 12 are under a constitutional obligation to act reasonably and without any arbitrariness even in the matter of contract ..... the health insurance contract is related to the category of life contracts ..... all bargains of insurance need not result in profit ..... a health policy, though under an annual contract on payment of annual premium, the assured must have a right of renewal subject to reasonable conditions, because the policy is not intended to be for a term certain, but meant to cover risk of disease for life so long the renewal premium is paid in time;

- NC: Manoj Jha vs. Unitech Ltd. ..... a term of a contract will not be final and binding if it is shown that the consent to the term was not really voluntary but was given under a sort of compulsion on account of the person giving consent being left with no other choice or if the term amounts to an unfair trade practice;

- SC: Pioneer Urban Land Infrastructure Ltd. Vs. Govindan Raghavan ...... a contract or term is substantively unfair if such contract or the term is in itself harsh, oppressive or unconscionable to one of the parties;

- NC: Veena Khanna vs. Ansal Properties Ltd. ...... the consumer fora is not governed by adversary system procedure but by inquiry proceedings, and the State Commission ought to have looked into the substance of the matter and at the defence of the opposite parties.

The reader will no doubt bear in mind that these are only excerpts. One should Google / web research and imbibe the full import of these and other judgments, e.g. by typing, for instance, "SC in V. Krishna Rao", or something like "SC on consumer protection act + judgments", etc.

It may now be profitable to also add to our armoury a few Latin legal maxims:

- Eiincumbit probation, qui dicit, non qui negat: ..... the burden of proof lies upon him who asserts and not upon him who denies;

- Ignorantia facti excusat ignorantia juris non excusat: ..... ignorance of fact may be excused but not ignorance of law;

- Lex specialis derogate legigenerali: ..... special law repeals general laws;

- Nullus commodum capre potest de injuria sua propria: ..... no person can take advantage of his own wrong;

- Qui facit per alium facit per se: ...... he who acts through another acts for himself;

- Res ipsa loquitur: ..... the thing speaks for itself;

- Suppressio very or suggestion falsi: ..... concealment of truth or a statement of falsehood;

- Injuria sine damno: ..... infringement of a right is enough to be actionable;

- Jus natural: .... laws that an average person would find reasonable;

- Malum in se: ..... a universal wrong or evil regardless of the system of laws in effect;

- Per minas: ...... a defence when illegal acts were performed under duress;

- Ambiguitas contra stipulatorem est: ..... an ambiguity is most strongly construed against the party using it;

- Boni judicia est ampliare jurisdictionem: .... it is the part of a good judge to enlarge his jurisdiction;

- In sodium: ..... jointly and severally;

- Naturalia negotii: ...... express or implied terms that go to the root of a contract's subject matter;

- Restitutio integrum: .... to restore a party to an original position;

- Force majeure: .... an act of god / events over which no humans have control and, hence, cannot be held responsible;

- Contradictio in adjecto contra proferentem: .... ambiguous term in a contract shall be interpreted against the party that insisted upon the term's inclusion;

- Stare decisis: .... the obligation of a judge to stand by a prior precedent;

- Verba Volant, sed scripta manent: ..... spoken words fly away, written words remain;

PART TWO

CHAPTER FIVE

How to write your complaint

Writing a complaint to the consumer court is quite simple and easy. However, there are a few things to keep in mind: keep your complaint simple and to-the-point. Be truthful, don't suppress or misrepresent. Avoid bombast, personal attacks, and verbosity. You must bring out all relevant issues and supporting documents that are required to prove your case in the complaint itself. If you fail to do so, you may not be permitted by the court to resort to same in later stages of the proceedings. And do not forget to sign and date the complaint at its end.

You will require three sets for the court, plus a set each for each of the opposite parties, plus a set for your own records. You can very easily do it by yourself if you can do a bit of typing. Do so in double space, and leave sufficient as well as appropriate margins. The sample presented here below is representative; you can be creative as per the needs in your case.

BEFORE THE Hon'ble CONSUMER DISPUTES REDRESSAL COMMISSION

at ....(District), ... (State)

Case # .... / 2021

Mr. / Ms. XYZ .... Complainant
(complete address)
VERSUS

1. Mr. / Ms. / M/s. .... Opposite Party # 1

(complete address)
2 . Mr. / Ms. / M/s. .... Opposite Party # 2
(complete address)
COMPLAINT u/s 35 of the CP ACT 2019
It is respectfully submitted as under:
Opposite Party # 1 is the e-portal. The Opposite Party # 2 is the seller on the e-portal of the Opposite Party # 1. (Amplify if / as necessary).
<u>**COMPLAINT**</u>

1. I purchased a laptop on 08/02/2021 for Rs. xxxxxx from / via the OPs as per their invoice at **page** .....The said laptop was covered with 1 year onsite warranty, digitally produced at **pages** ....

2. That the said laptop stopped working well within the warranty period. I tried to reach out to the OPs for repair / replacement / refund, as digitally produced at **pages** ......herein, but there was no proper response from the OPs.

3. As I was in urgent need for a computer for my work, I was left with no other option but to make alternative arrangements by purchasing a replacement computer, in total costing Rs xxxxxx as digitally produced at **pages** ....

It is respectfully submitted that not complying with s/4 of The Consumer Protection (e-Commerce) Rules, 2020 Of CPAct to provide proper and timely resolution to consumer issues amounts to Deficiency in Service and Unfair Trade Practice. It is submitted that giving wrong address in invoice is Deficiency in Service and Unfair Trade Practice. It is further submitted that the post sale deletion / removal of the seller pages / details / product details from their e-portal is Deficiency in Service and also Unfair Trade Practice. It is submitted that failure to correct such and various shortcomings despite flagging amounts to negligence on the part of the Opposite Parties, and they are jointly and severally liable for costs, expenses, damages, exemplary damages for the unwarranted mental, physical, and financial loss / harassment / trauma caused to me, and for making me unnecessarily run around courts.

PRAYERS: concerned OP #s jointly and severally:

a. Direct OP # 2 to within seven days to conform to s/4 and other provisions of The Consumer Protection Act, (e-Commerce) Rules, 2020;
b. Take back the non-working laptop and make good the Rs. .... spent on alternative –replacement purchase;
c. Costs of Rs. ....;
d. Miscellaneous expenses of Rs. ....;
e. Rs. xxxxxx each compensation for the negligent unwarranted mental, physical, and financial harassment;
f. Exemplary damages of Rs. xxxxxxx each;
g. Any other relief thought to be fit and proper.

COMPLAINANT
(date, month), 2021

Make an index of the contents and their locations, as per representative sample below, and attach same at page # "0" of the complaint:

BEFORE THE CONSUMER DISPUTES REDRESSAL COMMISSION

at .... (District), ... (State)

.... / 2021

Mr. / Ms. / M/s. .... Complainant

VERSUS

Mr. / Ms. / M/s. &ors. .... Opposite Parties

INDEX

Content Page #s

1. Cause Title & Background ....

2. Complaint ....

2. Invoice, Legal Notice, & evidence documents ....

COMPLAINANT

(date, Month), 2021

CHAPTER SIX

Admission of the complaint by the court

After the complaint is lodged by you, it will be allotted a complaint number. The court clerk will check that the names and address of complainant as well as of the opposite parties have been provided, the complaint has been signed and dated, and the requisite number of copies have been supplied, and so on. You will then be given a date for "admission". This entire process will typically take less than ten minutes.

During the admission hearings the court will verify for things like correct geographical and pecuniary jurisdiction, and the appropriateness of the reasons for your complaint. This entire process would typically take less than ten minutes.

Upon the complaint being admitted, the court will then issue a date, or an extension thereto if so necessary, directing the opposite parties the opportunity to file their Written Statements / Reply to your complaint.

CHAPTER SEVEN

Written Statement by the Opposite Parties

This is almost always a mechanical process. The opposite parties will file their Written Statements and furnish a copy of same to you, or they may seek an extension to do the same. The courts will then grant an extension of 15 days for completing this aspect of the process.

Filing of Affidavit-in-Evidence

You had filed your complaint to which the opposite party brought on record their version by way of their Written Statement (WS in short).

The next step is for you to file your Affidavit-in-Evidence. That is to say, you are to bring on record the evidence documents and whatever you say under oath / affidavit and thereby vouch for their veracity. This Affidavit-in-Evidence (AE for short) is essentially a recap of the complaint combined with elements of rejoinder / rebuttal to the WS that was filed by the opposite party.

A representative sample of an AE is shown here below. But remember, the AE and its evidence documents must, repeat must, be verified and sworn by you and must be so done under oath before a notary. This simply means that you take the AE to the notary and put it under oath by signing it and putting a date at the bottom before the notary. The date of signing should be the same as the date on which it was notarised. In other words, let the notary complete its process wherein they themselves will put in the date, i.e., the date of signing the oath. As for the evidence documents contained therein, the ones that are based on hard copies of things like invoice, correspondence, brochure, etc., and you have their originals, these too need to be notarised for authenticity. This is much like notarising a copy of a driving licence, or Aadhar Card, or mark-sheet, etc. But those evidence documents need not be notorised that originated digitally, but you should mention this fact in your AE.

BEFORE THE CONSUMER DISPUTES REDRESSAL COMMISSION

at .... District), ... (State)

28 / 2021

Mr. / Ms. .... Complainant

VERSUS

Mr. / Ms. / M/s. .... Opposite Party

EVIDENCE AFFIDAVIT

of

COMPLAINANT

I, Mr. / Ms. ...., s/d/of Mr. ...., aged .... years, manager, and manager / housewife / doctor / car mechanic / (etc.), residing at .... do respectfully say under oath that:

1. I say that whatever I have said in my Complaint is true to the best of my knowledge and belief and, unless specifically traversed and specifically admitted by me, everything stated by the Respondents in their WV would stand as denied and / or refuted and / or not be tantamount to acquiescence.

2. I respectfully say that it is not correct for the OPs to say that the matter involves complex issues of law and facts for the following reasons .... I say that mere production by the OPs of repetitious and / or irrelevant documents and

averments, and interjecting same into the matter does not make the matter a complicated one; ...... what it makes for is a garrulous compilation designed to confuse issues and mislead / confound the Commission. Be that as it may, I say that somehow the OPs have not disclosed the relevant information that .... I further respectfully say that, be that as it may, the issues are simple and straightforward of Deficiency in Service and Unfairness: why have the OPs not complied with s/4 of The Consumer Protection (e-Commerce) Rules, 2020 Of CP Act, as well as its other provisions / why has the OP # 1 not resolved the various issues flagged by me on several occasions as digitally produced at **pages** ....herein.

3. I say that it is not correct for the OPs to say that I am not a consumer. I say that I am neither the manufacturer nor the seller, nor do I buy and sell these products for commercial use, but solely to earn my livelihood by means of self-employment as will be seen from the digitally produced copy of my ITR at **page** ....herein.

4. I deny that I have wilfully withheld any relevant information or that I am wrongfully harassing the OP. Rather, the OP has wrongfully refused to reimburse my medical claim bill of Rs. xxxxxxx on the specious grounds that I did not submit the necessary documents. I say that not only I had submitted the necessary documents, but that the OP had duly verified and receipted same as per the notorised evidence **pages** ....,herein.

Or, something like:

I had purchased and paid in advance for the tyre / computer / fan / shoes / (etc.) as per the digitally produced evidence documents at **pages** ....,herein. However, upon receipt of the product it was found that the MRP on the box was shown as Rs. 100 as at **page**

........herein, whereas the OP has wrongfully overcharged Rs. 105 which is above the MRP.

I say that, over a period of many months, I have been flagging issues / making efforts for resolution, but to no avail. I respectfully say that despite such flagging by me, not complying with s/4 of The Consumer Protection (e-Commerce) Rules, 2020 Of CP Act, and its other provisions, by the OP amounts to Deficiency in Service as well as Unfair Trade Practice. I say that not resolving consumer complaints on a timely basis and / or selling above MRP, or wrongfully refusing to reimburse my mediclaim bill, etc., as outlined elsewhere herein above amounts to Deficiency in Service as well as Unfair Trade Practice. I further say that failure by the OP to correct such shortcomings amounts to negligence, and that they are jointly and severally liable for make good the same, and are also liable for costs, expenses, damages, exemplary damages, for making me run around courts and causing me unwarranted mental, physical, and financial loss / harassment caused to me.

VERIFICATION

I, Mr. / Ms. ...., s/d/of Mr. ...., and aged .... years, Indian, and manager / housewife / doctor / car mechanic / (etc.), residing at ...., do hereby verify and state that what is stated by me in my affidavit herein is true to the best of my knowledge and belief.

Verified at (Place): , 2021.

COMPLAINANT

AFFIDAVIT

I, Mr. / Ms. ...., s/d/o Mr. ...., and aged ..... years, Indian, and manager / housewife, doctor / car mechanic / (etc.), residing at ...., do hereby say that what is stated by me in my affidavit herein above is true to

the best of my knowledge and belief.
Verified at (place): .... , 2021.
DEPONENT

Affidavit-in-Evidence by the Opposite Party

This also is almost always a mechanical process. The opposite party will file their Affidavit-in-Evidence and furnish a copy of the same to you. The courts will then give a date on which to file your Written Arguments.

Written Arguments of Complainant

The written arguments are the reiteration of what you have said thus far in your Complaint and Affidavit-in-Evidence, and debunk whatever the Opposite party has said thus far in their Written Statement and in their Affidavit-in-Evidence. Here, bring into play and use logic to its full extent. Deploy metaphors, biting sarcasm, dry humour, light hearted analogies. But don't get personal, and don't go overboard. This is the right place for you to bring into play all relevant precedent judgments in support of your arguments, and put to rest those of the opposite party.

A representative version of a Written Arguments is shown here below. One should tailor it to one's own case circumstances and needs.

BEFORE THE HON'BLE CONSUMER DISPUTES REDRESSAL COMMISSION

at .... (District), ... (State)

Case # .... / 2021

Mr. / Ms. XYZ (Senior Citizen) .... Complainant

VERSUS

M/s. ABCD Ltd. &Ors .... Opposite Parties

WRITTEN ARGUEMENTS

of COMPLAINANT

It is respectfully submitted that:

1. The issues raised in the complaint are inter-related / linked / twined, with the insurers being the fountainhead whence two streams flow: the one at Respondent # ...., their TPA hired by them, AND the other at Respondent # ...., the hospital, over each of whom they have superintendence in matters of quality, quantity, costs, with corrective powers of de-empanelment / administrative / legal enforcements.

2. The insurers and their TPA have, from time to time, made payments against claims, presumably on the basis of documents submitted to them by the complainant. BUT, off-and-on they had been denying parts of claims on the specious grounds that this or that document was not submitted to them by the complainant, even in the face of evidence submitted by the complainant that such documents had, in fact, not only been duly submitted by him to the opposite party, but these were duly verified and receipted by them. The said Respondents have not produced or placed on record any evidence to the contrary to support their purely verbal assertions, and are, therefore, accountable to make good their Deficiency in Service and Unfair Trade Practice.

3. On a number of occasions via email and also by way of personal representations the various false / fabricated billings, as evidenced in affidavit, indulged in by the Respondent hospital were brought to the notice of the insurers. Such false / fabricated billings caused losses not only to the complainant but also to the insurers

themselves. However, other than mere verbal assurances and a post-office type email, there was no corrective action taken by the insurers to remedy the unfair trade practices indulged in by the hospital, which makes the insurers themselves to be in negligent Deficiency in Service and Unfair Trade Practice.

4. The hospital respondents have relied upon purely verbal representations. Nowhere have they adduced any evidence that "mysterious" and un-required, and non-provided "special" nursing services were prescribed by my doctor or, for that matter, even provided at all. Ditto for dietician, which in any event, is part and parcel of hospital costs, just like a thermometer, or receptionist, or accountant is. Similarly, the hospital Respondents, OR, for that matter the insurers, have not produced any evidence to show that Dr. XYZ's consultation fees were Rs. 700 as wrongfully billed, and not Rs. 300 (at that time) or Rs. 500 at present as notorised evidence produced by the complainant. Neither the hospital Respondents, nor even the insurers, have adduced any evidence that carotid Doppler test was Rs. 7000 as wrongfully billed by them, and not Rs. 2200 as notorised evidence submitted by the complainant. Neither the hospital Respondents, nor even the insurers, have explained as to why such huge wrongful inflated costs are charged to an insurance patient. Further, the hospital charged for catheter that was never brought into use for the patient, nor did they provide some of the medicines billed. The hospital also billed for things like masks, gloves, keeping records, etc. that are part and parcel of hospitals own cost structure.

However, the key issue here is that whereas the hospital is in Deficiency in Service and Unfair trade Practice for their false / fabricated / inflated billings, WHAT effective remedial / corrective steps have the insurers and their TPA, those who speedily jump to strike down petty Rs. 4 costs for gloves, etc. put up by the patient, but turn a Nelson's eye to the Rs 1000's wrong / false / fabricated / inflated billings put up by the hospital ? ....are they not in negligent nonfeasance / misfeasance / as well as malfeasance amounting to negligent Deficiency in Service and colluding in Unfair Trade Practice? ... and should they not be held to account in terms of **SC: Lucknow Development Authority vs. MK Gupta,**

"..... should the society or the tax payer be burdened for oppressive and capricious act of the public officers or it be paid by those responsible for it."

" .... Who should pay the amount determined by the Commission for harassment and agony, the statutory authority or should it be realised from those who were responsible for it? Compensation as explained includes both the just equivalent for loss of goods or services and also for sufferance of injustice. "

" .... A public functionary if he acts maliciously or oppressively and the exercise of power results in harassment and agony then it is not an exercise of power but its abuse. No law provides protection against it. He who is responsible for it must suffer it. "

" .... it should further direct the department concerned to pay the amount to the complainant from the public fund immediately but to recover the same from those who are found responsible for such unpardonable behavior by dividing it proportionately where there are more than one functionaries."

" .... it is further directed that the Lucknow Development Authority shall fix the responsibility of the officers who were responsible for causing harassment and agony to the respondent within a period of six months from the date a copy of this order is produced or served on it. The amount of compensation of Rs 10,000 awarded by the Commission for mental harassment shall be recovered from such officers proportionately from their salary."

It is respectfully submitted that the respondents are jointly and severally liable for their negligent acts / omissions of Deficiency in Service AND Unfair Trade Practice and, hence, my complaint may be allowed as prayed in my complaint.

COMPLAINANT

(Place): .... (Date), (Month), 2021

CHAPTER ELEVEN

Written Arguments by the Opposite Party

This too is almost always a mechanical process. The opposite party will file their Written Arguments and furnish a copy of the same to you. The courts will then give a date for "orders / judgment", in which case the proceedings are complete. Await a certified copy of the orders which is supplied free of cost by the court.

PART THREE

CHAPTER TWELVE

Be forewarned and forearmed

"It all depends on the judge" or something akin to that is what I was told by more than one advocate I had approached some years ago to represent my case before the consumer courts. "Wait a minute, why should it 'depend on the judge' when I am in accordance with the law, and when I have all the required evidence?" The answer to this question was cruelly shone on me down the line at the school of reality. I hasten to share such knowledge with you, by way of the "case study" method, of ground reality, so that you are not taken by surprise by events that may unfold during the course of the proceedings.

Several years ago I had filed a case against a prominent industrialist - builder group. Unfortunately, the "judge" turned out to be one that was very aggressive and arrogant to the point that I was obliged to cross legal swords with him in a couple of instance before a full courtroom. He recorded in the roznama that he could not understand what the complaint was all about, when it was clearly mentioned in my complaint, with all supporting evidence documents, that despite having paid in full on time, the builder was refusing to register the flat and transfer it to my name;

the area of the flat delivered was less than the promised; the electric wiring was defective giving sparks with loud sounds at the main distribution board; the bathroom tiles were not of the requisite non-skid type; and that there was no demarcating boundary wall or the free parking space in contravention of the law. During the next hearing the judge demanded that he should have an on-site physical verification of my allegations, and we arrived at the flat during the court lunch hour. He huffed and he puffed, but I demonstrated to him the defective sparking and mini-explosion type sound emitting from the main electric distribution board. He then switched off the power and demanded that I show him the same again! When told that he had switched off the power, he then went to the bathroom and said that the builder had provided floor tiles so why are you complaining? When I retorted that should one not complain if a car was delivered to me with bicycle tyres instead of regular car tyres, he cut short the meeting and left. I knew I was in trouble as the judge was trying this or that way to derail my case. Fortunately, I was not the only one dissatisfied by the style and substance of this judge and, after some research, a case was filed against him in the High Court for corrupt practices in his employment terms. When a couple of hearings were splashed across the local media, this judge resigned and left. I was hopeful that the next in line presiding lady would be competent and fair. I was sadly proven wrong. She allowed the opposite party three consecutive adjournments without recording reasons in writing or imposing costs as per law. When I verbally raised this issue she became agitated, and continued to do more of same. I recorded my protest by way of registered mail, whence she became even more hostile and aggressive, at which point I lodged a complaint with the High Court,

Law Minister, Department of Civil Supplies, etc. A few days later a copy of reply letter to my complaint directed enquiries against the said errant presiding member. Around this time her tenure was also due for renewal, to which I objected as her being unfit. Mercifully, she quit and left. My complaint was progressing when the next judge arrived. I must say he was calm, and listened. However, his body language started to trouble me when, for instance, despite my matter typically being listed at the top as for a senior citizens, he would relegate me to the very last when the courtroom was empty. After coming to a reasoned assessment, I wrote to a friend that even though he likely would not rule against me because the law, evidence, and records were overwhelmingly in my favour, he was likely to word his judgment in such a manner as to be detrimental to me and favour the opposite party. This is exactly what he went on to do. I had prayed either for the flat to be made to conform to all laws and contractual terms, or to be provided an alternate similar flat in the vicinity, or to be refunded per prevailing market price. Instead, however, he allowed refund with 15% interest which caused me a huge loss as property prices had gone up many fold, by far more than the 15% interest. He did allow me punitive damages of three lakh as a show of his "fairness" in the case. But shockingly there was not a single word in his judgment as to why he has allowed a refund with 15% interest and not prevailing market price as prayed, and why he imposed the three lakh punitive damages on the opposite party! This case took five years.

In another case the District Commission granted me a lump-sum compensation of one lakh. In appeal by the opposite party the matter landed up before the same bench as above in the State Commission. I applied for the judge to recuse himself, and he did, although under much protest from the other members of the bench. To cut a long story short, the bench obtained its pound of flesh by dismissing my case as frivolous and imposing costs on me. Again, not a single word by the Commission as to how it came to the conclusion that my case was frivolous in the face of overwhelming photographic and written evidence produced by me, and not opposed, or even denied, by the opposite party. Or why it found the District Commission award in my favour to be erroneous. How, in hindsight, I wish I had instituted a complaint against the bench, but getting old with health issues, I decided to not to do so, and move on in life. The case was decided on time in maybe three months.

By this time in the reading the gentle reader may be inclined to throw in the towel. But don't, for there are many good judges and courts too out there, and contrast the next two instances here below with the two above.

Some fifty years ago I put in a request for my provident fund monies from Mumbai to Delhi. The officer refused to do so unless I supplied him Vitamin "C", which vitamin I don't do. The matter was agitated by me in the High Court before the bench of the late Justices Rajinder Sachar and Leila Seth. The two or three responding parties did not file their Written Statement on the first date, nor on the second, not even in the third, on which occasion the bench was livid with something like: have you heard of a phone, do you know of something called an aeroplane, what about a telegraph .... if you have anything to say at all, say it by the next hearing or else return his provident money. The bench then proceeded to give a date of next hearing for one week later. Lo, and behold, on the next hearing I was given my provident fund money by way of a Pay Order! The case was disposed off in a matter of just two or three months.

A few years later I had reason to file a Writ Petition against SEBI. The two or three respondents failed to file their Written Statement even after four or five dates over a period stretching for more than a year. I was dismayed and requested my advocate to withdraw my petition, to which he suggested for me to wait for another date or two as there would be a new judge. The new judge immediately took severe note of the tardiness of the respondents and warned of very harsh consequences. The matter was resolved by the OPs before the next hearing, and I withdrew my writ. The case was settled in a little over a year.

It will be seen from the above illustrations that it does indeed "depend on the judge".

A judge typically is vested with sufficient powers to be able to effectively, efficiently, and in a fair manner adjudicate matters under his charge. Over and above he also commands considerable moral authority. And whereas there are many efficient judges out there that are to be welcomed like manna from the sky, one may, on occasion, encounter the type that will deploy his energies towards the hole in the doughnut rather than towards the doughnut itself by wrongful granting of adjournments, not recording or incorrectly recording the roznama, by seeking repeated clarifications, by issuing orders that are without reasoning, and so on, which unfortunate situation will require the negotiating skills, as like with a chance encounter with a leopard on the street.

In short, don't pray to have the best lawyer in the world to represent you; pray only for a good judge, because even though you may not have the best lawyer, or may even be representing yourself, a good judge knows that he is there to dispense justice in accordance with the law, and not there to engage in avoidable technicalities. He will come prepared before the hearing starts, will correctly and efficiently deploy his knowledge of the subject, and guide the matter along, without favour to you or to the opposite party.

CHAPTER THIRTEEN

What to do in the event of ......

In the unfortunate event you are caught in proceeding that are not as per law, you should first raise the issue before the court itself. If that does not work, one can put up an application to the effect and place same on record. If that too does not work, you may consider doing same by registered post. And if that too fails, a written complaint under affidavit with supporting evidence documents can be made to the concerned department under which the consumer courts function, or to the Chief Justice of the relevant High Court, or to the Chief Justice of India in the Supreme Court. Your grievances can also be raised with the Department of Justice, the Law Minister, the Prime Minister, or even the President of India. But be very brief and to the point.

One can obtain useful guidelines on the subject on web sites like:

https://doj.gov.in/sites/default/files/GUIDELINES.pdf

https://menrightsindia.net/2017/05/how-to-complain-against-judge.html

https://indiankanoon.org/search/?formInput=complaint%

https://main.sci.gov.in/pdf/cir/
2014-12-31_1420006239.pdf
https://districts.ecourts.gov.in/Ecourtktm16-0
cindiankanoon.org/
search/?formInput=misonduct%20by%20judicial%20officer
https://www.duhaime.org/Legal-Dictionary/Term/
JudicialMisconduct

CHAPTER FOURTEEN

A few Rx observations

We strive for improvements, towards which end some suggestions are tendered here in the hope that someone or the other will consider them;

- Many of the cases could be disposed off within the suggested three to five months provided that the provisions of the CP Act are adhered to, unwarranted adjournments are eschewed, and the next dates are at shorter intervals of say five to ten days.

- The normal hearing hours of the Consumer Commission are 10.30 a.m. to 1.00 p.m. and 2.00 p.m. to 4.30 p.m. It has been my experience and observation that commencement of proceedings at such late morning ensures avoidable loss of a half working day for almost all litigants, and even a loss of a full working day for some. Even otherwise we are a tropical country, and commencement of hearings at 9.00 a.m. to 1.00 p.m. would go a long way to ease the burden on the litigants. The afternoon session can be for the utilised for the purpose of writing judgments or administrative work.

- From my experience and observations in the Consumer Commission where I am present, the proceedings often or even invariably conclude by 11.30 a.m., and only very rarely go on till the allotted 1.00 p.m. Yet, many matters, especially arguments, are avoidably left off midway and adjourned to another date.

- The matters by or against senior citizens, handicapped, and widows are to be listed on priority. However, this stipulation is not always adhered to. It could be considered to set aside, say 5% of proximate dates, for speedier listing of cases by or against senior citizens, handicapped, and widows.

THE END